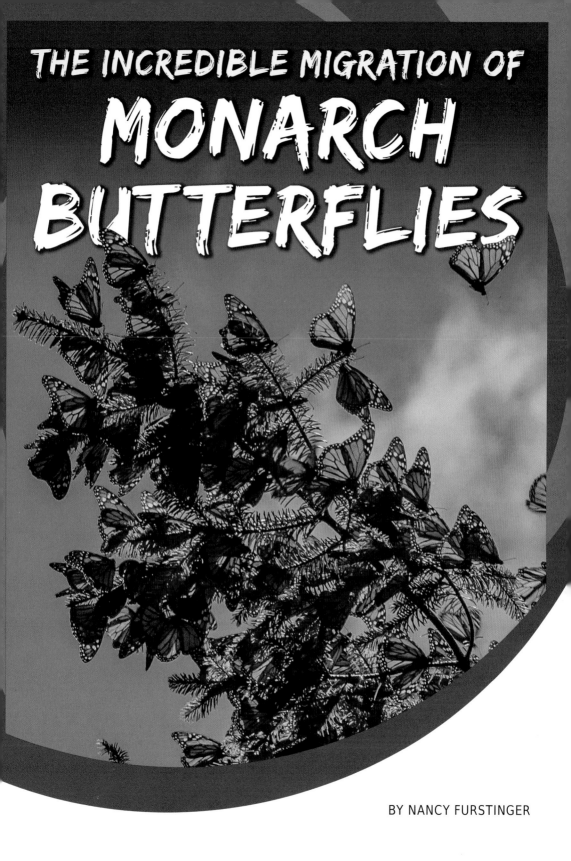

THE INCREDIBLE MIGRATION OF MONARCH BUTTERFLIES

BY NANCY FURSTINGER

The Child's World®
childsworld.com

Published by The Child's World®
1980 Lookout Drive • Mankato, MN 56003-1705
800-599-READ • www.childsworld.com

Photographs ©: JHVEPhoto/Shutterstock Images, cover, 1; Red Line Editorial, 5; Elizaveta Kirina/Shutterstock Images, 6; Holly Wilmeth/SIPA/Newscom, 8; JHVEPhoto/iStockphoto, 9; Cathy Keifer/iStockphoto, 10; Thomas Kitchin & Victoria Hurst/Glow Images, 13; Perry Correll/Shutterstock Images, 14; True Nature/Shutterstock Images, 17; Nick James Stock/iStockphoto, 18; Kyle Daly/USFWS, 20

ISBN 9781503816190

LCCN 2016945619

Printed in the United States of America
PA02319

TABLE OF
CONTENTS

FAST FACTS

Name

- Monarch butterfly (*Danaus plexippus*)

Diet

- Monarch caterpillars feed on milkweed plants.
- Monarch butterflies drink **nectar** from flowers.

Average Life Span

- The first three generations live two to six weeks.
- The fourth generation lives six to eight months.

Size

- A monarch's wingspan reaches up to 4 inches (10 cm) wide.

Weight

- Monarchs weigh up to .026 ounces (.74 g).

Where They're Found

- Monarchs live in fields, meadows, and woodlands.

- In summer, they range throughout North America down to South America.

- In winter, monarchs east of the Rocky Mountains **migrate** to the Monarch Butterfly Biosphere Reserve in Mexico. Those west of the mountains migrate to the California coast.

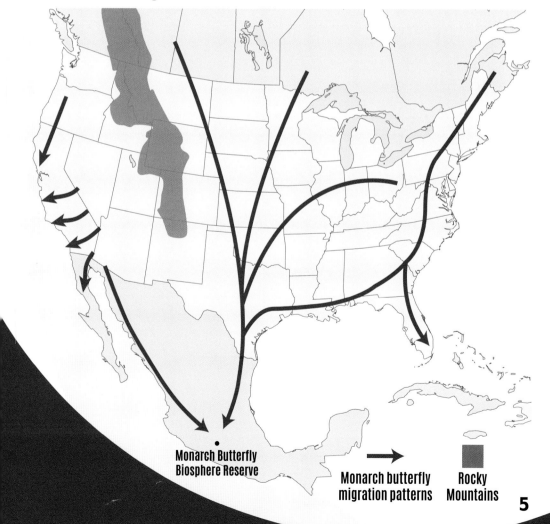

Monarch Butterfly
Biosphere Reserve

→ Monarch butterfly migration patterns

▮ Rocky Mountains

Chapter 1

A BLAZE OF BRIGHT ORANGE

Rays of afternoon sunlight peek down into a forest in Mexico. Suddenly, rustling fills the air. A swirl of orange rains down from the sky. The swirl swoops toward a fir tree. In seconds, the tree is no longer green. It blazes bright orange.

Thousands of monarch butterflies cluster together. They stretch out their wings to soak up the sun. Their wings look like stained glass windows. They are a dazzling orange with black lines and white spots.

Schoolchildren walk through the forest. They have come to see the gathering of butterflies.

◄ The Mexican government created the Monarch Butterfly Biosphere Reserve in order to protect migrating monarchs.

▲ The migrating monarchs attract
many visitors.

A guide from the Mexican government carefully leads the schoolchildren down a path. He explains that the butterflies have just completed a long migration. They have traveled thousands of miles to reach this forest in central Mexico.

The monarchs settle on the fir trees around the group of schoolchildren. The guide explains that this helps the monarchs keep warm as temperatures drop in the evening. Monarchs cannot live in the cold. That is why they migrate.

Some of the butterflies have traveled for two months to make it to the forest. Here they will be safe for the winter.

▲ Monarchs do not eat while they are wintering in Mexico, but they do drink water.

Chapter 2

FLYING SOUTH

The monarch's great journey begins in the fall. The days grow shorter and colder. The adult monarch knows it is time to migrate. Soon the weather will be too cold for her. She needs to fly south for the winter.

The monarch flaps her wings and takes off. She zooms through the air at speeds up to 30 miles per hour (48 km/h). The monarch is plump from drinking nectar from flowers. She will need the energy for her long trip south. When she gets tired, the monarch spirals upward on an air current. Then she glides through the air while her wings take a rest.

The female uses the rising sun to guide her migration. The sun is to the east when she flies in the morning.

◀ **Migrating monarchs drink lots of nectar from flowers in order to make the long journey south.**

Later in the afternoon, the monarch flies with the sun to the west of her. Soon the female joins with a flock of monarchs. They are going south, too. None of them have migrated before. But they know how to use the sun as their guide.

Far below, the female spots a mountain range. She follows the ridges south. Thunder rumbling in the distance interrupts her trip. The monarch is caught in a sudden storm. She has a difficult time flying with raindrops pinging off her wings. She finds shelter in a tree to rest with her small flock. When the rain stops, she sips nectar to gain energy.

The monarch takes off but faces a new danger. A hungry bird swoops down. It bites down on one of the monarch's wings. The bird quickly releases the butterfly. The monarch tastes terrible to the bird. The monarch continues to fly south with a tiny piece of her wing missing.

Because monarchs do not weigh much, large raindrops can ▶ knock them off course and even cause injury.

Chapter 3

A NEW GENERATION

After two months of travel, the monarch flutters into the mountains in central Mexico. She floats down onto a tree branch. Thousands of other monarchs also **roost** in the tree. Their weight bends the branches down to the ground. Throughout the winter, the monarch lives off the fat she has stored.

Eventually the days grow longer and warmer. Spring arrives. The monarch finds a mate. She flutters around, searching for milkweed plants. Milkweed has big, broad leaves. It is the perfect spot to lay her eggs. She lays nearly 700 eggs on milkweed plants over a few weeks. Each egg is about the size of pencil tip.

◀ Female monarchs usually lay their eggs on the undersides of milkweed leaves.

Soon after laying her eggs, the female monarch dies. But the monarch migration continues.

After four days, the eggs **hatch**. A green **larva**, or caterpillar, wiggles out from each egg. The caterpillar is hungry. First she eats her eggshell. Then she eats the leaf the eggs were attached to. She eats other leaves, too. Soon the caterpillar becomes too big for her skin. She **molts**, or sheds her skin. The caterpillar now has a new layer of skin. It has bold yellow, black, and white stripes. She molts five times. She grows to be 2 inches (5 cm) long.

Once she has eaten enough, the caterpillar attaches to a twig. She forms a hard casing around herself called a **chrysalis**. Inside the casing, the caterpillar turns into a butterfly.

A bird looking for food passes by the chrysalis. It does not spy the casing because it is **camouflaged**. The **predator** is tricked into thinking the green casing is another leaf.

▲ A green chrysalis underneath a leaf is difficult for predators to see.

After two weeks, the casing cracks open. An adult monarch crawls out. Her wings are tiny and weak. The butterfly hangs upside down. She pumps fluid through the veins in her wings to make them grow bigger. The butterfly waits two hours for her wings to harden. Soon she will be ready to fly.

Chapter 4

COMPLETING THE CYCLE

The second generation of monarchs begins the trip back north. On their way, they stop often to drink nectar. This keeps their strength up. But this generation has a much shorter life span than the previous generation. The adults will live for only two to six weeks. The monarchs have two jobs to complete in this time: fly part of the way north and lay eggs.

The migration north is like a relay race. Each generation of monarchs flutters closer to their summer home. Finally the third generation arrives as milkweed starts to bloom in the north.

◄ **Soon after the second generation of monarchs emerge from their chrysalises, they begin the journey north.**

▲ Many people help monarchs by growing milkweed.

But as they fly, some of the monarchs have a difficult time finding a safe place to lay their eggs. Farmers have plowed under the milkweed meadows near the monarchs' summer home. Instead of flowers, fields of corn now sway in the breeze.

20

Luckily, the monarchs spy a garden behind a school where milkweed blooms. The butterflies swoop down to lay their eggs.

In late summer and early fall, the fourth generation of monarchs hatch. These butterflies will live up to nine months. They will make the long trip south for the winter. They are the great-grandchildren of the monarchs that made last year's journey. It is their turn to start the cycle over again.

THINK ABOUT IT

- Why do monarchs need to migrate south each fall?
- How is milkweed important during the different stages of a butterfly's life?
- How does the monarch's migration north resemble a relay race?

GLOSSARY

camouflaged (KAM-uh-flazhd): To be camouflaged is to be hidden or disguised. Animals can be camouflaged by different colors and patterns that blend into their environments.

chrysalis (KRIS-el-es): A chrysalis is a hard casing that protects a butterfly while it is turning into an adult. The green chrysalis blends into the tree from which it hangs.

hatch (HACH): To hatch is to come out of an egg. Caterpillars hatch and then eat their eggshells.

larva (LAR-va): A larva is a young insect that hatches from an egg. The larva of a butterfly or moth is a caterpillar.

migrate (MYE-grate): To migrate is to move from one place to another. Each autumn, monarch butterflies migrate to their wintering grounds.

molts (MOLTS): Something molts when it sheds its outer covering and replaces it with new growth. A caterpillar molts when it outgrows its skin.

nectar (NEK-ter): Nectar is a sweet liquid produced by flowering plants. Butterflies drink nectar to build up fat.

predator (PRED-uh-tur): A predator is an animal that kills and eats other animals. A bird is a predator of a butterfly.

roost (ROOST): To roost is to settle down for rest or sleep. Monarchs roost in trees in the forests of central Mexico.

TO LEARN MORE

Books

Gregory, Josh. *Monarch Butterflies*. New York: Children's, 2016.

Hirsch, Rebecca E. *Monarch Butterfly Migration*. Mankato, MN: The Child's World, 2012.

O'Sullivan, Joanne. *Migration Nation*. Watertown, MA: Imagine, 2015.

Web Sites

Visit our Web site for links about monarch butterflies: childsworld.com/links

Note to Parents, Teachers, and Librarians: We routinely verify our Web links to make sure they are safe and active sites. So encourage your readers to check them out!

SELECTED BIBLIOGRAPHY

Hiles, Sara Shipley. "Green Scene: Little Migrating Miracles." *Defenders of Wildlife*. Defenders of Wildlife, 2016. Web. 2 Aug. 2016.

"Migration." *Monarch Lab*. Regents of the University of Minnesota, 2016. Web. 2 Aug. 2016.

"Monarch Biology." *Monarch Watch.org*. Monarch Watch, n.d. Web. 2 Aug. 2016.

"Monarch Butterfly Biosphere Reserve." *UNESCO.org*. UNESCO World Heritage Centre, 2016. Web. 2 Aug. 2016.

INDEX

ABOUT THE AUTHOR

Nancy Furstinger is the author of more than 100 books. She has been a feature writer for a daily newspaper, a managing editor of trade and consumer magazines, and an editor at children's book publishing houses. She lives in upstate New York with a menagerie of animals.